THE BLUE MIRAGE

The Blue Mirage

ANNIE WILLIAMS

Annie Williams

The Blue Mirage

"What is this?"

An illusion that I thought was real,
Mixed with a fantasy that I want,
But obscured by a nightmare I fear.
Questioning my sanity,
As I proclaim profanity,
While I drown in dazes of blue,
From the darkest of midnight,
To the coldest of ice,
Parts of my mind are tainted.
Other parts are masked up beauty.
I know deep down I'm living in lies,
But am I prepared to face the truth?
Will the truth ever equate to my lovely imagination?
Will the truth be more terrifying than the evil in my head?
What shade will I turn into when I seek the truth?
Will I turn into a soft baby or dive into the ultramarine?
Will I become a royal or fly to the sky?
Will I be striking like electricity or dull like steel?
What will I collapse into at the end?
Or will I find a new shade that is perfect for me?

"Where do we go?"
"Who shall we be?"
"What is our true hue?"

Almost Paradise

Classic Cult

The sunlight creeps through the broken window,
And slowly crawls up the short white dress worn by a beautiful girl.
Her dark curly hair hangs down in a mess as she twirls around,
With the sunlight kissing her soft mocha skin.
She spins, jumps, and falls as if she's in her own world,
Smiling and laughing with every clumsy step,
With a large audience of boys wearing wolf masks watching.
They circle around the girl and watch her in awe,
And all of them wonder how a beautiful angel like her landed in a hellish world.
They never get bored with the way she moves,
And she loves the violence they create to those who think of her in vain.
They plot sacrifices and crimes just to have a chance to hold her,
And they hope that she will never fray too far away from them.
Fortunately, she would never think of it,
Cause she knows they can't survive a second without her,
And as long as they are loyal to her and only her,
She will continue to dance for them,
But if any one of them disregards her kindness,
The other boys will start a riot in her name.

Thunderstorms in Winter

Dark clouds roar,
Lightning flashes across the sky,
As snow gently falls,
Kissing the grass,
And brushing the white coat of a wolf.
The wolf walks all alone on this stormy winter day,
With the lightning illuminating the snowy terrain.

Crash

Lightning flashes again,
And it hits a giant oak tree,
Setting its old branches ablaze.
The white wolf stops in its tracks,
And sits in front of the grand fire,
Watching the wood crackle,
And ashes gently kiss the ground,
Just like the snow falling from the thunder clouds.

Cold Skin

Without you even knowing,
You are haunting me,
Keeping me awake till sunrise,
And sending shivers down my spine.

You have possessed me to love you madly,
And I need you so badly,
But even though I belong to you,
You will never belong to me.

Frostbite

He said I gave him the chills,
By staring at my cold eyes,
And trying to see through my icy heart.
Although he's freezing,
He says many stars have burned him
And he is sick of all the scars,
So he's starting to appreciate the cold.

Artthrob

He is great at painting,
Good at the guitar,
Can hold a note,
Always wears that old denim jacket,
Got that soft brown hair all the boys and girls adore,
And always says he's a nobody surrounded by
somebody's',
Yet wherever he goes eyes turns,
Whispers ask about him curiously,
People are hooked on his every word,
But he doesn't realize it,
Because he's busy dreaming away,
Using his guitar and paints to escape reality.

Higher

Will you fly away with me,
And help me find something new?
I've been tired for some years now yet can't sleep,
And I notice all those pills you take doesn't provide you
the comfort you keep asking for,
So why don't we pretend we aren't strangers today,
And maybe I'll gain affection for you,
And you may or may not reciprocate it back,
But let's see where we can go from here.
Let's drop all these damaging people in our lives,
Let's pretend that we were just born,
And let's run innocently into something new.
I'm sick of this never-ending cycle,
And I know you are as well,
So will you fly away with me,
Or am I wrong,
And you do like living in a state of emptiness?

Empty Boy

I know nothing can make you whole again,
But I want to help you become fuller.

Kisses Kills

I could love you for life,
But I'm afraid I'm in strife,
In trouble with my past,
And terrified we might move too fast,
Yet I still can't get my mind off you,
And I want your feelings to be true.

Playful

In a crowd of hundreds,
With beautiful bodies and faces,
You still stare at me,
Trail your curious eyes up my skirt,
And wish for me to be your baby,
But you misunderstand me.
Although I'm melting inside,
I'm gonna give you an icy stare,
And act innocently ignorant,
Because I love making you go crazy,
And adore watching your eyes fill with sin.

Sweetest

You're my cup of tea,
My harmony,
A lovely lullaby,
That feels as good as a cry.

Spacious Love

I could gift you the earth,
Let you have all the seas and land,
With all it's rough edges,
And smooth terrain.
The earth can be yours,
And only yours.

I could gift you the moon,
Let you dance in its light,
Or even play in its dark,
Run around the rocky surface.
The moon can be yours,
And only yours.

I could gift you the sun
Let you feel it's fire,
Swim in its hot lava,
And own the greatest star.
The sun can be yours,
And only yours.

I could gift you the earth,
I could gift you the moon,
I could gift you the sun.
I could gift you the universe,
But still the universe is quite small,
Compared to the love I have for you

Shooting Star

If I could be granted one wish,
I would ask for us to not end like this.

Fatigue

Won't you lay me down to rest,
And sing me a song to calm my mind.
I don't know why but I'm exhausted,
Even though I haven't done much today,
My body feels heavy,
And I have no energy.
I wish I could give you a reason why,
But I can't hear my thoughts clearly.
So please won't you sing me to sleep,
And please don't be too mad when I wake.

Three Answers

"What are dreams?"

"They are what drive people."

"Our secrets we don't want to admit to ourselves."

"Ways to say hello to passed loved ones."

A Beautiful Dream I Had

In a dream,
I saw you.
I don't remember what happened,
Where we were,
Or if anyone else was there,
But I felt your presence,
Saw your pale as snow face,
Wearing your dark clothes.
It truly was you I believe,
And I was so happy to see you,
But then it all went away fast.
I woke up and was still in bed,
And you were still high above the clouds.

My Cries

If I yelled your name,
Would you come running into my arms?
Or would you cover your ears,
And ignore my screams of love?

Unreality

Only have twos bucks in my coat pocket,
And there is no one to text or call.

No interesting places to go,
Besides, the gas in my car is running low.

It's alright though.
I know a place that I don't have to drive to.

I can go whenever I like,
And it doesn't require a long hike.

It's filled with people I want to talk to,
And to top it all off it's free.

I can do whatever I want there,
And I can easily breathe the air.

It's a wonderful place.
A wonderful place called my imagination.

Dream of Us

We are dancing in my head,
With you in a suit meant for a king,
And I wearing a gorgeous gown of blue.
I rest my head on your chest,
As you hold me in your strong arms,
Wanting to never to let go of me,
And hoping the night lasts forever.

Bitter Bite

Come and digest me,
But first dissect me.
Know what you're getting,
Before you try me,
Because if I start to like you,
My feelings will surely devour you.

Timeless

Sick and tired of sitting in my bedroom,
I went outside and took a walk.
It was a little after midnight,
The sidewalks were quiet,
And I had no clue where I was going,
But my feet knew exactly where to take me.
After 10 minutes of strolling along,
I found myself by the old docks.
Moonlight glistened on the quiet waters,
And no one was around it seemed.
Not even some pesky seagulls,
Or maybe some old creep,
But then down at the end of the docks,
I saw them.
It was a foggy pair of people,
Swaying together in underneath the moonlight.
It was a young man and woman.
The man was wearing a tattered up vintage suit,
With a small hat on top,
While the woman was wearing some kind of flapper
dress,
With a long boa around her neck.
Their faces were so young,
Yet they were so old.
All they did was slow dance with one another,
Acting like nothing in this world can bother them.
For some reason,

I was so drawn to them.
I couldn't help but stare at them.
For a second I wanted to approach them,
But their scene seemed too perfect to ruin.
Buzz
My phone then buzzed,
Probably a text from a friend,
I thought to myself,
So I checked it.
Just a notification from Twitter.
I only looked down for a second,
But when I looked up they vanished.
Nobody was at the end of the docks.
Disappeared in an instance,
Without leaving any trace except in my head.

Too Much

I wonder where you are,
Because I need to breathe you in like a cigar,
Take you up into my lungs,
And taste your poison on my tongue.
I want to be forever by your side.
I'll even stick with you if you commit homicide,
Because darling you bring me sanity,
And you make me believe in humanity.
You are my long-lived remedy,
And if you ever left it would be the greatest tragedy.

A Lovely Death

Oh love of my life,
Come to me quickly,
Kiss me passionately,
And embrace my boulders of feelings.

Strangle me in your comfort,
And make my heart beat so fast it stops.
I want to die in your gentle arms,
And leave this world in happiness rather than madness.

Foolish Love

Maybe you knew him,
And maybe I didn't,
But I loved him like nobody else could,
And maybe while nobody should.

Dialogue Between My Parents

"How are you doing?"

"I'm fine...don't worry. What about you? Are you ok?"

"...If you're not ok, then we are not ok."

Magical

Pink skies,
Singing birds,
And tulips dancing in the sunlight.
Air so fresh,
And a land so beautiful,
But no royals in this fairy tale.
There's only people with broken minds here,
Rolling around in the flowers beds,
Laughing and smiling for the first time,
Breathing without their lungs fluctuating,
And jumping around carelessly in their weightless
bodies.
Just living well now that their hearts have slowed
down,
And happy to not deal with wicked villains anymore.
Now they are here tasting happiness for the first time.
All they do is dance with the tulips,
With the birds singing,
Underneath the pink skies.

DIVINE

An angel fell from heaven,
But wasn't welcomed to hell.
So she was thrown to the earth,
With broken wings and a nose running blood.

She walked clumsily through the world,
Peoples' eyes locked on to her and stared,
Watching her stride in gracefully clumsy steps,
Like she was walking on broken glass.

Although her bare feet burned every step,
She continued walking because there's nothing else to
do.
She walked through dirty streets buzzing with people,
And forests that only sang still silence.

She went down ancient dirt roads,
Saw flowers playing with the wind,
And many strange creatures up close.
After miles and miles she found herself on a quiet
beach.

It appeared not a single soul was around,
And the sun was falling fast asleep.
She breathed in the salty air as she looked around,
But then she lost her breath when she saw a figure on
the far side.

It was a blurry red figure she couldn't make out.
Her wings shivered at the sight,
But after remembering the predicament she's in,
Nothing worse can happen to her now.

She walked the beach to reach the figure,
Thinking maybe it's just another human,
Or possibly just an illusion she has made,
But as she got closer she was able to see.

The figure was sitting in the sand,
His bright red skin soaking up the sun,
Sharp horns sticking out of his dark hair,
And even darker eyes staring out to the waters.

He was a demon taking a break from hell,
And feeling sick of all the idiots he has to deal with.
Sitting there all alone smoking a blunt,
Hoping the boss man won't be too mad at him.

Then he hears the rustling of sand next to him,
And looks over to see a tattered angel.
Although her skin was rotting gray and covered in
bruises,
She was the most beautiful creature he has ever seen.

The angel looked down at him with an icy stare,
And she stood there still like medusa saw her.
The demon smokes out a puff and asks,
"Why are you down here?"

Why am I down here?
The angel thought to herself,
But then she remembers how she was given the right to
choose,
But her choices didn't make Heaven so happy.

The angel let out a heavy breath,
And calmly as she can she says,
"It's none of your business,
But why are you in this world?"

The demon lets out a small laugh,
"Hell is full of idiotic assholes."
"Well, Heaven isn't that great either,"
She replies with a small grin.

Smokes leaves his lips,
As he asks, "Care to sit?"
The angel sits down in the sand,
Right next to the demon.

The demon passes the blunt to her,
And she gently takes it out of his hand.
She copies the way he smoked,
Bringing it to her lips and taking it all in.

She takes in too much,
And she coughs a little.
The angel passes back the blunt,
And the demon laughs a little.

With a mischievous grin he asks,
"Are you ok?"
The angel looks out to the waters with a smile,
"I've never been better."

Belle Mort

While walking on the old creaky bridge,
On a beautiful spring day with the birds chirping,
I saw a lovely lady floating in the river.
Her skin whiter than a ghost,
And brighter than the sun,
Floating down the river with frogs croaking,
And crocodiles brushing past her.
She passed underneath my feet,
And drifted to the other side where all the lilies lie,
Sleeping safe and soundly in serenity.

"What Do Souls Sound Like?"

I could talk to you all day,
From soft whispers to high shouts,
But I can never hear your voice,
When you're all the way up in the clouds.

Total Chaos

Where Is Peace?

I want to live a peaceful life,
But the stars weren't aligned,
And my head is filled to the brim with tar,
So much so it leaks through my ears,
And is burning me inside out.

I Know Her Best

Enna is such a beautiful girl,
And many people say she's sweeter than honey,
But to me she's bitter to the bone,
And the cruelest person I ever met.

Although such a pretty face,
Behind that mask is a selfish girl,
With a twisted mind,
And a weak back.

She's one of the worse people I know,
So idiotic and stupid,
Serves no purpose,
And has a fragile heart.

Every day she spits her ugly truth to me,
But I spit right back at her,
Tearing at her flesh,
And yelling curses at her.

I hate her.
Always will so long I breathe,
And I'm filled with disgust knowing her,
And more disgusted when I lock eyes with her in the
mirror.

Deception Of The Mind

You've been showing up in my dreams,
Kissing me passionately,
And holding me tightly,
Doing what I wish would happen if we reconnected,
But I know in reality you would look at me coldly,
And even if you still had feelings for me,
You have someone else to kiss and hold.

Shadows

Truths in the dark.
Lies in the light.
All the words you say
They feel so right.
Even though I know this is an illusion,
I prefer to see this than have sight.

My Play

Let me be honest for once,
And call myself a filthy liar.
I lie to you and say everything is good,
I twist myself to be doing better than I am,
Pretend I am actually living instead of breathing,
Act like this reality is just my imagination,
But all the bad things are real,
The devil is knocking on my door,
I don't know where any angels are,
And I am dancing on a thin tightrope.
A tightrope hovering over hundreds of spikes.

LOVEHATEHATELOVE

The want for love has corrupted me,
Infected my whole body,
Invested in me like hungry roaches,
Eating away at my mind,
Making me constantly dream it,
But at the same time,
 it frightens me.
Giving someone the key to my locked heart,
Allowing him to fill it with gasoline and burn it,
Or he fills it with joy and makes every moment
memorable.
Either way,
 I hate it.
Terrified of it,
Because one way he destroys me,
Or gets me falling at his feet.
Either find someone else to replace me,
Or we live happily together until life takes him.
In the end,
 he will leave,
Yet humans are meant to love right?
Then why in the end we split up no matter what?
Why can't I be alone like how I'll end?
Being alone forever sounds much safer than giving
everything I am to someone,
Yet I've been craving affection,
Some type of adoration.
Although it scares me,
It's a nightmare I can't help but fantasize.

Committed

You could spoon-feed me glass,
And make me choke on my blood,
But my heart will still beat for you,
And I would say you didn't mean it.

"Can You See?"

Don't look!
He's looking at you,
So is all his friends,
And everyone in this room.
They are all looking at you,
Judging the way you look,
Whispering malicious things about you,
Noticing how you tick at your fingers,
Hearing your breath get heavier and heavier,
And thinking how stupid you are.
Trust your mind,
Listen to me,
Don't look!

Quiet Coward

Have my earbuds in,
With one blaring song on repeat,
As I look down at my dirty shoes,
And try my best to pretend I'm somewhere else,
But I can't help think that someone is staring,
Judging the way I breathe,
Whispering everything that's wrong with me,
Yet their thoughts about me can't be as ill as my own.

Rain In Late December

December 29th -

Rain splattered on the window,
Shaking the empty house,
But I still laid motionless in my bed,
Wishing I could do something,
Maybe call an old friend,
Or read a good thriller,
Or clean my cluttered room,
Or take that shower I've been putting off,
But even thinking of it is tiring.
Although I do want to get up,
It seems I don't have enough strength.
My mind says I'm lazy,
Saying I'm so pathetic,
And I think it's' right,
Although my heart and body feels tired,
I do want to get out of this uncomfortable bed.
I want to rip through these blankets and sheets,
And start watching all my favorite movies again,
Begin reading all the books I once adored,
See my friends again and meet new people,
And I want to truly be alive rather than just an
existence.
Not just a stranger to everybody.
Not just a ghost passing by.
Not just a memory easily forgotten.
I want to move,
And I want to breathe,
But my head is pounding.

My body is exhausted.

My heart is aching.

Nothing seems amusing.

Everything feels like a chore.

Getting out of bed is quite difficult.

All of this makes me tired,

But at the same time,

 I can't feel anything.

I can only feel my house shaking from the pounding rain.

Stubborn

Tears are building up,
But I refuse to show you any,
Because I rather you think of me cold and heartless,
Instead of think I am fragile and vulnerable,
And let you use that to your advantage.

Intimate With My Demons

Abyss wraps his claws around my throat,
As he sits on top of my locked up chest,
And sings me a lullaby that makes my blood coil.

hush

I've been crying so hard I'm breathless,
Yet I've become so numb I couldn't feel the tears.

Emily

Emily kept a skeleton in her bed,
Dressed up in a suit and tie,
While she always wore her dress.

As she laid next to him,
She would play out their perfect wedding,
Imagining their kiss underneath the altar.

Every day she would pretend to be happy,
Listen to the love song they would dance to,
And spend her day with the dead.

MEANDI

I killed her,
WIth my bare hands.
Her neck snapped like a twig,
And she fell in my arms.
All I could do is laugh.
I've had thought of it thousands of times,
Gone through so many plans in my head,
But I finally went through with one.
Maybe now everything will be better.

I killed me,
With my bare hands,
My neck snapped like a twig,
And I fell into my arms.
All I could do is smile,
But then I woke up.
Dreaming of those thoughts again,
Thinking if I did it everything will be better.

Bandaids And Sleeves

I'm sorry mom,
I knew it would scare you,
And I'm sorry dad,
I knew it would worry you,
But the razor kept calling my name,
And I must have blackout,
Because I don't remember getting all these cuts,
And I have forgotten again I am not paper.

"You're My Best Friend,

Don't You Know That?"

We've known each other for a few years now,
You seem to enjoy being around me,
And once you called me your friend,
But I'm always the one to reach out to you,
While you're never the one to say hi first,
And many times have treated me like a ghost,
Especially when you're around your other friends.
Then when you do acknowledge me,
It's to get something from me,
And you always say you'll pay me back,
But you're in debt.

Stranger Danger

There's a stranger living in my house.

He looks so similar to me,
Got the same last name,
Knew me since I was a baby,
But I know nothing of him.
I've only seen him yell or destroy.

There's a stranger living in my house.

He has nowhere to go,
Can't leave the state,
Can't even drink with that tether on.
He can stay here since my mom knows him well,
But when I hear his footsteps I'm scared as hell.

There's a stranger living in my house.

He always says he's doing better,
And although I avoid talking to him,
I can tell he's lying through his teeth,
Choking down the truth of his turmoil,
And pretending he's in control.

There's a stranger living in my house.

I don't know much about him,
Try to hide my emotions towards him,
But I feel sad when I see him drunkenly cry,
Angry when the police calls again,
And frustrated when he's using grandma again.

There's a stranger living in my house,

Every time I see him I tense up,
My heart breaks bit by bit,
I feel guilty for hating him,
Yet can't bring myself to love him.
I wish I could see him differently,

But I only see a stranger living in my house.

Teeth Marks On My Tongue

I've been chewing on my tongue like it's bubblegum,
And counting to 1,000 in my head,
Looking down at the scratches on my desk,
And wishing for the day to be over,
Because I feel so uncomfortable with the thought of someone looking at me,
And jittery inside with the idea of someone talking to me.
I don't want to be here,
But I already missed too many classes,
And I'm a little worried about the consequences of what would happen,
Yet so scared of what the day will be like.
At home,
Or in class
Or in a store,
Or in a crowded party,
Or even alone I feel nervous about something.
Over worrying about what each hour will bring me.
Even if nothing is currently wrong I get uneasy.
No matter where I'll go I'll be uncomfortable.
So I'll just continue chewing,
Continue counting,
And stare into space,
Hoping no one stares back.

The Sickness

My bones aren't broken,
My nose isn't running,
My heart must be beating,
Yet I can't feel it.
My senses haven't been working in a long time,
And I can't feel or taste anything anymore,
Yet I'm fully aware of my empty stomach,
And how heavy and dark my eyes are.
So heavy even with eight hours of sleep,
And so dark even though there's light peeping through
the curtains.
There's a light trailing over my eyes,
But it doesn't feel warm,
And it doesn't look bright either,
It's just there.
Everything is just here.
Such as I who is just here.
Walking around the earth,
Watching everyone pass me by,
Not batting me an eye.
I'm just breathing here,
But a lot of times it's even hard to breathe.
Like my lungs are collapsing,
And the walls around me are closing in,
But it's easier to breathe in bed,

So much easier when I'm hiding under the covers,
Yet can't get comfortable with my unsteady mind,
But I just stay in it.
Stay by myself,
Doing absolutely nothing,
And being absolutely nothing.

The Watchful Princess

I was sitting in my glass castle when I saw the world go red.

My beautiful glass castle that only fits me,

And nothing else can enter my sanctuary.

Although my skin is untouched my eyes saw it all.

I saw knights break through each others' armor,

Horses drop to the dirt when a screech rings in the air,

And children crying as they hide from the battlefield.

Then the sky started to cry with them,

And raindrops splashed into the puddles of blood,

But my glass castle didn't let anything in,

My skin wasn't stained like the hundreds of bodies outside.

Only my eyes were stained from the grotesque scene,

Yet I did nothing and enjoyed my silent glass castle.

Death Wish

I see a white star in my backyard,
Floating beautifully in the black night,
Glowing brightly with thunder clouds roaring.

The white star notices how dull my eyes are,
And it calls out towards me,
"Let me show you something better than this!"

For a second I'm scared,
But then like a cheetah preying on an antelope,
I exit my house and chase towards the white star.

The sound of thunder and pounding rain echoes,
As I run through the wet grass,
And get closer to the light.

Once I reach the white star,
I swear it looks at me,
As I slowly reach out
To embrace its warmth.

Crash

I saw a white star in my backyard,
Now my soul is floating on Jupiter
While my body lays on earth,
Surrounded by the dust of my other life.

Useless

There was an earthquake on Mars
And I could hear screams from the stars,
Shouting their curses,
Yelling violent verses,
Erupting in cries,
As tears overwhelmed my eyes.
Then comets crashed into each other,
Killing one another.
All this so frightening,
As striking as lightning,
Yet I can't look away,
And I just softly pray,
Hoping it may do something,
Do anything,
But I know this universe is already broken,
And disaster has already spoken.

Standing In The Scorching Sands

Calling all my angels on tonight's summer moon,
Please come to me with all your might and grace,
And take me away from this hot island of isolation.
I need to go before the bright sun explodes across the
universe,
And burns every little last good thing I have.
Please come before the mermaids of my past start
calling my name,
And drag me into the trenches to try to kill me again.
Hurry please because I'm afraid of what's going to
happen to me,
And more afraid that I won't care anymore what will
happen to me.

Send Me Away

God send me a train,
And I'll wait on the tracks.

Oh universe strike me with a disease,
And I'll embrace it lovingly.

Dear world bring a serial killer to me,
And I'll give him a clean knife.

Come and do the worst to me,
And let me breathe for once in my life.

Rid me of myself,
And send me away to paradise.

Dawn Of A New Age

Sirens rings across the red sky,
As the ocean starts to ripple,
And the ground beneath my feet tremor.
The ocean starts to pull apart,
While everyone runs as fast and far as they can from
the beach,
But I stay to watch like the fool I am.
The ocean pulls further and further apart,
Thunder starts to roar,
And something pitch-black starts to rise up;
Horns made of rubies pokes through the water,
Bright white eyes glow,
And a large black shadow stands.
Taller than the Eiffel Tower,
And as wide as the titanic,
The giant stands still for a second,
As the beach screams bloody murder.
I look up at the shadow,
And he looks down at me,
Piercing his gaze through my body,
Trapping my feet in the hot sand,
And leaving me breathless in its horror.
The giant shadows looks out to the world,
And lets out a violent screech,
Before his reign of terror commences.

GREED

He tore through my clothes and skin like it was mere
   paper.

   His hands were stained from ripping through my flesh
and bones.

   He felt all my skin and muscles and took it all.

   He painted his lips with my crimson blood.

   He devoured everything I was in a heartbeat,

   But after the slaughter he still wanted more.

Body On The Shoreline

The beach sand sticks on my skin,
The waves crash upon my lungs,
The sun burns my prune face,
The seagulls pick at my flesh,
And the crabs crawl on top of me,
As I scream like a banshee,
Yet my mouth doesn't move an inch.

Beyond The End

My body fell to the floor while I was ripped away from
my flesh,
And I saw some luminous lightning flash before my cold
eyes.

All the reds, blues, pinks, oranges, greens, purples,
yellows, blacks, browns, whites,
And every other color I ever knew disappeared in an
instant.

At first, I was terrified of this awakening to the other
plane,
But now with no running blood, I feel lighter than ever
before.

All I can feel is this overwhelming sense of
everythingness,
And I feel my soul erupting like a star in this dark plane.

Floating in between the end of the beginning,
And the beginning of the end.

Tasting this atmosphere of euphoria so critically,
While I flutter through all the moments of my former life.

Thinking about the people who will be joyous or ill when they find out what happened,
And holding close to my heart the names and faces of the ones I truly loved.

Dreaming of all the memories I felt that are impossible now to ever touch again,
And hoping that maybe someone will remember me as I strongly remember them,

Yet I feel ready to go beyond everything that I ever known,
And I will allow this death to comfort me in ways I never thought it could.

It Does

It shouldn't bother me,
But when the worm got in my skin,
Eating away at my flesh,
It's hard to pretend the pain isn't there.

Dead Air

I try to talk to you,
But you're always busy,
So I always tell you,
"Just text me whenever you can,"
But that was months ago,
And suddenly you're back,
Acting like we are best friends,
And now I'm wondering if I should try again,
Finally have someone close again,
Or if I should stay in my lonely room,
Because I know it never disappoints.

Where Were You?

Ignored me all my life,
And acted like I didn't exist,
But now that I'm gone,
You're acting like you cared,
And we knew each other so well.
May I ask where all this love was when I was here?
Because now you're wasting it all on my dirt,
Talking about all these memories of us that don't exist.

Perfect Doll

My plastic skin has been perfectly shined,
My hair has been done to your liking,
Got my pretty cherry lips on that you adore,
Have the dress you picked out on,
And I am completely painted to you desires,
But you still keep playing with other toys,
Complaining that I'm broken,
But won't tell me what's wrong with me,
And keep me latched to your side,
Refusing to let anyone else near me.
You just see me as your prize,
While you are the cause of my demise.

ENNA

I see her now,
In my house of mirrors.
I see her now,
Without her plastic mask on,
Staring back at me,
With paper eyes two different colors,
One green,
Other orange,
And nothing else on to show her body of tar,
Yet I see myself in her.
I see her fragility,
Feel her emptiness,
Hear her loud silence,
And taste her icy stare.
I see her in all my mirrors,
Staring back at me.
I want to look away,
Cut my eyes open,
Pour in clean water,
And wash out the filth I've seen,
But I know I can't keep running.
I can't no longer pretend we are not each other
anymore.
I want to run towards her,

Go through the glass,
And strangle her with my bare hands,
But at the same time,
 I want to hug her,
Tell her maybe we will get better.
Hell maybe apologize to her,
But for now,
 I can't.
So for the best,
 I'll look at her,
Study her a bit,
Try to understand why she's like this,
And maybe one day I'll accept her:
Her and all her wretchedness,
And maybe see what's so pretty about her.

Gotta Go

Just like everybody else I got close to,
They are moving away.
They move into nicer places,
Or on to new faces,
Or move into a new existence.
I want to shout at all of them,
Be the selfish soul I am,
And ask them why they have to leave?
Did I do something wrong?
Why couldn't they have stayed?
I'm mad at them all for leaving,
But most of the time it's not their fault.
Life decided to put them in my life for a reason,
And life decides when they shouldn't be part of it
anymore.
The world will forever keep turning,
New and old people will come into my life,
And then walk out one way or another.
The only person that will stay with me is me,
And I must still be in this world for a reason.

Real Life?

River Of Change

On the bridge of innocence,
Crumbling underneath my feet,
And going to drop me in the fast waters of the real
world,
Where I will either drown under the heavy current,
Or I'll swim gracefully as a koi fish,
Going strong in one direction,
Still unsure if I'm heading to the fall,
Or to a pretty pond of pearls.

Know Your Place

Look at you.

The world has poisoned you,
And made you into an ant.
An ant crawling on the dirty floor.
No one notices you,
And when they do
They step on you.
You've been living like this for a while now,
And I know you say it doesn't bother you but that's a
lie.
You have become used to being seen as small and
feeble,
And you allow them to tear you up like a chew toy,
But dear you are so much more than that.
You can feel it in your soul,
You are capable of much more,
And you deserve so much more than the world has
given you.
You deserve love, joy, and success,
But the world blinded you with dirt.
It's time to wash yourself,
Clean yourself a new,
And show your ever-glowing soul.
It's time to show your authentic colors.
And to evolve into a better you.
Don't let anyone stop your evolution.

The only other thing stopping your evolution is you,
But your evolution can start just by being you

Writing

When words wind up in my throat,
It's like I'm possessed by a ghost.
My body is overwhelmed with this urgency,
And I can taste the air so critically.
My heart starts to thunder,
And the words just bleed out onto the paper.
Before I know it hours passed,
And my hand is sore from stringing all these sentences.
Some of it doesn't make any sense,
But all of it had shed my heavy skin,
Made me feel lighter than a feather,
And I find myself breathless in the wretched beauty of words.

Full Bloom

I tasted the sun,
And it engulfed me in flames,
Burnt me to ashes,
Laid me in the dirt,
Where I blossomed into tulips,

Average Life

Working that 11-6 every weeknight,
Getting home to make some breakfast,
While his wife gets ready for that 10-7.
After he's done eating,
And she's done getting dress,
He drives her in their one beat down van,
Takes her to work and says goodbye with a quick kiss,
She gets to her job of helping bitter and self-entitled people,
While he gets back home to pick up the house,
Does a bit of laundry and some dishes till its about noon,
And he takes a short nap to wake up at 2.
He gets up to prepare an easy snack for his daughter,
Even though she's old enough to get something herself,
He always tries to spend time with her when she gets home from school,
By either watching her favorite show or telling each other inside jokes.
He still gives his time to his daughter when he should be spending time to rest,
But he has to do other things as well.
He has to do some grocery shopping,
Or fix up the car again.
Either way,

He has to give his time away to something.

After another hour he finally goes to bed for a few more hours.

Then he wakes up to pick up his wife.

On her feet all day,

Wearing those old gym shoes that are worn down,

She's exhausted from the mundane routine,

And sick of all the idiotic customers she had to deal with,

But when her husband picks her up she tries not to show it,

Because she knows he's running on 5 hours of sleep.

They get home to their daughter eating pizza rolls,

And a cat crying at their feet for more food.

They smile at her,

Spoil the cat some more,

Grab something to eat,

And enjoyed each other's company.

They watch some shows together,

And tell stupid stories they love,

Making one another laugh to death.

Then it's about 8,

And he has to go to sleep.

While he sleeps the wife does her share,

And picks up the kitchen and living room.

The daughter pitches in a little,

But her mom said she got it,

And will call for her if she needs help.

She never calls.

The daughter hangs out in her bedroom,

Feeling a bit useless to her parents,

And wishing she was more helpful.

She does her share as well.

She does the trash,
Put clean dishes away,
Vacuums the living room,
Does some laundry,
Cleans up the bathrooms,
And her parents said on top of all of that she makes them happy.
Trying her best in school and being a good daughter,
They say they appreciate her so much,
Still with those reassures she wishes she could do more,
Do as much as they do for her.
To help a little more,
At the stroke of 10 pm,
She checks to see if her dad is up.
He's up and moving,
And gets ready for his job.
The wife and daughter wish him a goodnight at work.
He tells them he loves them,
And they say it back.
Then he heads out the door,
While the wife and daughter heads up to bed,
Another day over for them,
While another night starts for him.

Spilled Blood

Look almost identical,
Yet share nothing in common.

Got similar blood,
But our hearts beat differently.

When I look you in your big red eyes,
You think I'm passing judgment on you.

Maybe it is judgment,
But my judgment never equated to hatred.

We hardly speak,
Just casual hi's.

When we do talk we are either awkward strangers,
Or we are both filled with tears cursing at one another,

I want to be close to you,
And I think you want to be close too,

But with you acting so reckless and angry,
And me not knowing what to say,

We just push each other far away.
So far away I sometimes forget we are related.

PURPLE

I am purple,
Simply a mix of red and blue.

Although a mix of red and blue,
I'm nowhere near red or blue.

I don't look red,
Yet they say I'm not truly blue.

They say I act too red,
But then say I'm trying too hard to be blue.

I feel a bit out of place with other reds,
But it feels I'm not welcomed by some blues.

They say I have too many friends who are red,
But they also say I hang out with too many blues.

It seems both sides don't fully like me,
And I feel a disconnect with my colors.

On the rarity I wish I could just be red or blue,
But I am not.

I am purple,
Simply a mix of red and blue.

Heartbreaker

I broke his heart,
While hurting my own.

I thought I was ready.
I thought I could be with him.

He said I could be the one,
And he wants to take a chance on me.

He knew this was a risk,
But I refused to let him take it.

He said he could see potential in me,
But what if that potential was a facade?

It truly wasn't his fault,
He's beautiful in every way.

So wonderful and sweet,
But I don't have the aptitude for romance.

He says he loves me,
Made the words sound easy to say,

But I can't say I feel the same way,
And don't understand how he's so fascinated by me.

It truly wasn't because of him,
So cliche to say but it's because of me.

I don't have the time or strength for love,
And I can't be with someone right now.

I mean how can I build a castle with him when my
footing is unstable?
How can I see a future with him when I'm still blinded
by the past?

I'm still struggling with a past love that will never
return,
So how could I be ready for another love?

I don't even know who I am,
And I need to figure out myself before exploring
someone else.

So the only way to end this is to be honest,
Even though honesty will be fatal this time.

Yes I feel strongly for him,
But I'm not strong enough yet for love.

So I told him that we had to stop,
But we can maybe be friends.

Of course he didn't like that idea,
And I sent him into shock when I said that.

Maybe I somewhat led him on,
But I always told him I'm not sure about us.

He said he understood,
But his eyes were so sad.

Now we haven't talked in a while,
And I do miss him,

But not miss him romantically,
I just wish we were friends.

I miss him,
But I know he needs his space.

I never wanted to break his heart,
But that was the only option in the end.

Because no matter how delicately I say the truth,
It will still stab him in the chest.

Maybe we would've been great together,
But right now I can't focus on love.

I still need time for myself,
And there's no room for love.

I broke his heart,
But I wish he never fell for me.

Because if he didn't love me,
Then maybe I wouldn't have hurt him,

And maybe we could've been friends,
But this is how we will end.

The finale of him being cut,
While my hands are bloody.

Bus Ride

20 degrees in January,
Waiting for the bus at 7 in the morning,
And we are freezing in the cold.
The bus turns the corner,
With big shining eyes staring down at us.
It rolls up to the curb,
And the door slowly opens.
The driver greets us with tired eyes as we climb aboard.
You sit in seat 13,
And I sit in seat 14,
On the opposite side of you.
We pass the time looking through the windows.
I see old oak trees and sleeping houses,
Along with soulless silent sidewalks,
While your sidewalk is filled with other kids,
Waiting or walking,
And you see wide awake gas stations,
And lively little stores.
My view is quiet.
Your view is loud.
My sights are dim,
And your sights are bright,
We see two different worlds,
Yet when the bus stops rolling,
We end up at the same destination,
Even though we had very different paths.

Kids No More

In elementary we were best friends,
Always played together at recess,
And then spend the weekends at each others' house.

In middle school we were friends,
Would sit next to each other at lunch and talk in class,
But we started to spend our weekends with other
people.

In high school we were strangers,
Had some classes together but never said hi.
When we see each other in the halls we act like ghosts.

Now close to graduation we are still strangers.
Strangers that have watched each other grow since 1st
grade,
Watching each other blossom as we distanced
ourselves further away each year.

Pandemic

People are fighting over toilet paper,
Buying food that can last for decades,
Staying at home as much as they can,
And running to the internet to forget a little,
Or read over the newest numbers of confirmed cases.
Schools are closed,
Parties are canceled,
The death toll is rising,
The elderly are sweating,
And the babies are innocent,
But their formula is being taken.
The president wasn't worried last week,
Said that everything is under control,
But now with cases of infection in every state,
He can't pretend no more he's in control.
Can't handle all this stress,
Even yelling at the reporters when they ask for some
comfort.
Everyone is blaming china,
Some are scared for Italy,
The spread is going fast.
Tens to hundreds to thousands.
Everyone is in a panic,
And I saw someone tweet,
"I never thought this would happen to me!"

Oh poor you I guess.
Then again I'm a hypocrite,
Because at first,
 I couldn't fathom it,
Didn't think it would come near my city.
Now it's here and so real.
I'm worried about my parents,
Hoping everyone is being safe,
A little bit scared,
But a bit more scared when I have to go to the store,
And I actually need toilet paper,
Unlike this person who's going to hit me for it,
Even though they have 50 rolls already.

Graduation

No caps or gowns.
No dresses or suites.
No games or assemblies.
No more of that.
Ended earlier than I expected.
Had my last hurrah before I knew it,
But let us all look back at those years,
And see how far we have come,
From the stupid teens we were,
To new adults entering the real world,
A world where a pandemic is going on,
But hope we all can make it through.

The Twinkling Star

Standing on my tiptoes,
I still couldn't reach the top of the tree,
And put up the twinkling star you love so much.

I grabbed a small stool to stand on,
And finally got the star on top.
It makes me realize how tall you were.

You could easily put the star on,
Hang the ornaments high,
And were my tall elf for the holidays.

We would get the whole house covered in lights before
night crawled around,
Just in time to watch a cheesy Christmas movie for our
guilty pleasure,
And for dinner we had hot chocolate with some
popcorn and cookies.

Now on my own I only got the Christmas tree up at 11
pm,
And I'm not hungry at all to enjoy any sweet treat by
myself,
And can't watch these wholesome movies with this
hole in my chest.

Yet I still can't sleep because I'm not comfortable with sleeping alone yet,

So I sat by the window to watch the snowfall for a bit,

And I ended up reminiscing about when we walked around the city with all its lights.

That night was freezing like Antarctica,

My bones were shaking from the frigid air,

But it was heartwarming to hear you say you loved me,

And even warmer when you kissed me when I said, "I love you too."

As I remember that night I looked up at the dark sky,

And in the emptiness I saw one twinkling star,

And I didn't know if I wanted to smile or cry,

When I thought it was you.

Blood Ties

When I could finally walk on my own,
My ears started to listen instead of hear,
And I could clearly see all your anger towards the world,
You thought I hated every single little thing about you,
But I can't hate someone that I don't know.

Another Night With An Addict

I was brushing my teeth when he came through the door,
And by his presence,
I knew he was on something.
He cornered me in the bathroom,
Asked me to help him with his new phone,
Because he just broke his other phone by throwing it out the car window.
I was scared of what he would do if I said no,
And I thought maybe it would be good for him to be with someone.
I hope maybe he will become more relaxed and get some sleep,
But he didn't.
He yelled at me when I couldn't figure out his phone,
Tried to get some more beer but tripped over his drunken feet,
Threw stuff around while yelling at the world,
And constantly asked me what I want him to do.
Kept questioning how he should fix himself.
I answer many times with,
"I don't know."
Or just the vague answer,
"I hope you get better"

He yelled at me for not knowing the answer,
So then I yelled the truth,
"I want you to get your shit together!
I want you to get your own house!
I want you to stop drinking all the time!
I want you to take care of yourself!
You're a grown man but you keep begging for money from mom and dad!
You use up grandma's bank account any chance you get!
You always say you make more money than mom and dad,
Then where is all your money?
Probably spent it on some coke and alcohol again!
I want you to stop playing the victim!
Always acting like you've been wronged,
And putting up this front that you're the good guy,
But good guys don't manipulate people to get money!
They don't constantly start fights with everybody!
They aren't selfish and egotistical!
They aren't you!
I just wish you weren't like this!
All I want is for you to get your shit together!
All I want is you to be a big brother to me!
I just want a big brother!"
The words echoed through the house,
But he didn't hear anything.
He yelled at me more,
And then he put on a pity show,
Crying his eyes out,
And then yelled at me to go to bed.
Mom and Dad came home at that time,
And there faces read,

"Not again..."
Dad went to talk to him,
While mom took me to her room,
And tried to comfort me.
All I did was cry,
And cry,
And cry,
And cry until I fell asleep.
The next few days I couldn't be in my house,
Because I knew he would be there.
So I would stay at school as long as I can,
And stayed at my aunt's house a lot that week.
After a little while,
 I saw him,
Tensed up by his shadow,
And the only thing he said was,
"I don't know what happened,
But whatever I did I'm sorry."
Like all the other times he blackout,
Doesn't realize what he has done,
And still doesn't realize that this isn't normal.

Holy Figure

He told me he wants to die at 33,
The same age Jesus died on the cross,
But the path he's going I don't think he'll make it to 30,
And unlike Jesus he's not going to rise up and be known as a savior.
He is just a broken man riddled with diseases in the head and heart.
When his body gets buried six feet into the earth,
My parents will remember him as a boy who always was in trouble,
His few friends will remember him as someone who did whatever he pleased,
While I will wish I could have known him better,
And I'll hope that Jesus will clean him at the gates.

Poisonous Love

I want to be your oxygen,
Make your life feel better in my arms,
But at the same time I want to suffocate you,
And make you cry as much as you made me.

Clear Sight

After fighting for your love countless times,
Giving you second chances left and right,
And trying to fix all the flaws you said I had,
My eyes have finally opened up,
And I can see nothing was wrong with me.
The only problem I had was you.

"I Want Something More"

I've fed you gold diamonds,
Took time to bathe you,
And wrapped you in warmth,
Yet you look at me with disdain in your eyes,
Forgetting all I've done for you,
But that is ok love.

Leave.
Go wherever you like.
Free yourself.
Runaway from my so-called nothingness.
Breakthrough from my comfort you call torture.
It's all fine love.

Nothing is stopping you,
So go whenever you like.
But when your pockets are empty,
And you get dirty and cold.
Don't come crawling back to my fire,
Because it will surely scorch you love.

Peeping Toms

Eyes are looking through the hundred holes in my house,
Watching me eat my bowl of shiny silver nails,
Drinking a warm cup of pigs' blood,
Letting it spill on my giant sheer white tee,
And trickling down between my thighs.
The eyes soak up the scene like a sopping sponge,
And I hear them whisper through the thin red wallpaper.
"What the hell is she doing?"
"What a waste."
"Something's wrong with her."
"So disgusting."
"How shameful."
"She must be ill."
"Inhumane"
"Nothing pure about her."
The other murmurs I can't pick up,
Because of how fast they spit,
Saying how damned I am,
Yet it sends their bodies shivering,
Got them drooling like a beagle,

Making their pants twinge,
And can't help but give in.
Must love watching me crumble like little sadists,
Must flip them on like a light switch to keep looking,
Must get them so high to talk,
Must be dreaming about me for spending so much time on me,
Yet never engages with me.
Just sits back and speak of me twisted,
As they watch like the cowards they are.

A Melodramatic Metaphor

Without my wishes,
I was thrown into the battlefield,
In a war constantly with my mind,
Feeling pain on my skin forever,
And tasting blood that made me empty.
I've met some great people,
Some who I've lost,
And some who just left me on the frontline.
Now I'm afraid to give anyone my trust.
My eyes were stained,
Innocence swept away,
And pieces of me broken.
Taking longer to heal than bones,
And more complicated than a cracked jaw.
I am now changed,
Changed from the happy soul I was,
To now playing chess with demons,
And trying to quench my thirst for fulfillment.
I thought maybe if I killed the one in the mirror,
Everything will feel better.
Rip away from my flesh,
And stop these screams in my head,
Make this sickness go away,
And be able to breathe again.
Maybe if my heart stops it will beat anew.
These thoughts swirl around me like a hurricane,
And these monsters echo them even louder,
But when I take a good look around me,
And see a boundless future in front of me.
I realize something.

Maybe there's a chance I will win this war.
Although so minuscule,
There's still that chance.
All this fighting must lead to something,
Whether one day my name be honored,
Or I die in happiness rather than madness,
Maybe I can get through the grime.
Dying joyfully seems much better than being killed by agony.
So for today,
I will not think of dying,
But instead of how I would want to die.
Die in a better place than this,
Keep going for myself and not for others,
Maybe reconcile with myself,
Find out what this glee feeling is that so many people have,
Hopefully find what is truly within me,
And not let these monsters in my head control me anymore.

Gods' War Cry

In the thunder clouds,
The dragons danced,
While mountains trembled,
And the sea froze in terror.

Tornadoes walked on the land,
Hailing fire in their cycles,
Setting the world ablaze,
And bringing everyone to their knees.

I AM

I'm my reckoning,
The villain in my story,
The monster in my bed,
And the killer of my dreams.

Yet I am my savior,
The knight that stands tall
The angel that flies high,
And the supreme in my dreams.

A Letter For You

Do you remember?

Because I do.

I remember when I first met you in third grade and I accidentally hit you with the dodge ball.

I remember when we were playing Left 4 Dead until 4 am and freaked out when we saw the witch.

I remember when you were struggling in school and I tutored you but it turned to eating lots of cookies and talking about idiots at school.

I remember when you were having a hard time and didn't want to be at your house so I let you crash at mine.

I remember when I had my first heartbreak and you let me cry on your shoulder and we colored and ate sweets.

I remember the last time I saw you and it was the first time we forgot who we were.

We looked at each other like strangers,

But I still remember you as my little sister.

I still remember all those fun summer nights at your house,

And the moments I heard you laugh and cry,

And our stupid fights and we didn't want to see each other,

But we always came back around because we are family.

Unrelated, different dna, unlike blood, but we are still family,

And I hope you always remember that,

Because you will always be my little sister.

The Runaway Kid

He's on the run,
Blazing like the fiery sun,
Only counting on luck,
And not giving a fuck.
Driving in his beat down car,
Hoping to go far.
He got no house or money,
Only drugs and a girl nicknamed Honey.
He believes he can escape reality,
Pretend he's in his own fantasy,
While breaking his family's hearts,
And using others by saying he's got a new start,
Lying through his tight clench teeth he's better and clean,
But he's been doing the same shit since he was 14.
Hurting his mom and dad,
Making his little sister sad,
Using his grandparents as much as he can,
And acting like he's The Big Man,
But all I see is a stupid kid.
A child that will never admit to all the damage he did,
Never will say, "I've caused this to myself,"
Blaming everyone but himself.

Hypocrite

He actually left.
I knew he would,
But deep down I wish he didn't.
So hypocritical of me,
I always wished he was out of my life,
But now he's probably never coming back,
And it's like I'm eating bits of broken glass.
I want him back.
I want to talk to him like everything is good,
Act like those annoying siblings I see on T.V.,
Pretend we have a bond instead of no bond,
And I wish this reality of mine was pure imagination,

But it is not.

The truth is that he's gone.
I didn't think it would hurt this much.
I thought it would be better if he left,
But it seems if he's here or there,
Next to me or miles from me,
A block or continents away,
Or on earth or among the stars,
Nothing is getting better,
And maybe all along I was wishing for the wrong thing.
Maybe I didn't want him to be gone.
Maybe I wanted his addiction to be gone.

Try Again

I've cried stars that have flood the darkest nights,
And I have renewed my broken wings to take flight.

I've been slowly rebuilding myself into a skyscraper,
And I refuse to allow anyone to crumble me like paper.

Two Worlds

Innovating faster than the earth can handle,
Creating beautiful digital cities that can hold millions,
And lets everyone be someone that they are not,
Living their most perfect life with their pretty masks
on.

While in the real world another school is gunned down,
There's blazing forest fires from hell,
People kill one another for their skin,
Or shoot someone for their belief or love interests.
Animals lose their home for more houses and buildings,
While the earth gets tired from carrying too many
people,
But it's ok.

Everything is ok because we have our other world.
Our dazzling digital destination,
Our sacred haven that can hold everyone,
Where we can escape from reality,
Forget for a moment all the tragedies,
Pretend we are doing better as a society,
While we avoid the real world and do nothing.

Healing

Yesterday I was afraid to be,
Didn't want to admit who I am,
But today I'm screaming my truth,
And never apologizing again,
For comfortably being myself.

Desolee

Je ne suis pas ce que tu voulais que je sois.

Je suis moi.

"I Will Always Be There For You"

"Where's Mommy?"

Lily looked up at me with those big blue eyes,
And she looked so confused.
Usually Serena would tuck her in,
And tell her a fairytale,
But now I have to,
And I have no idea what story to tell,
And I don't know how to tell her mommy isn't coming
back.
Then what if she asks where'd she go?
Am I supposed to tell her the truth?
Tell her mommy fell asleep on the hospital bed,
And she is never waking up?
Or should I tell her a lie?
Tell her that mommy took a long trip,
And she won't be returning anytime soon?
That's a horrible lie to say,
But the truth is unbearable to speak.
Should I break my little girls' heart now or tomorrow?

"Daddy?"

Oh Serena what do I do?
What would Serena do in this situation?

Why couldn't she be here?
Why couldn't it be like any other night where we had dinner,
Lily would make a mess of her food,
We struggle to get her to bed,
And then we go on the couch to relax.
Talking about our long days and boring jobs,
And have her in my aching arms.
Then maybe later in the night,
Lily wakes up from a nightmare,
And she crawls into our bed,
With Serena telling her there are no monsters,
And if there were to not be scared,
Because she and I were here,
And we would always be here.

"Daddy? Where's mommy?"

My eyes focused back onto her,
Back to her big blue eyes.
Those eyes she got from her.
My throat clenched up,
As tears started to fall.
I crumbled into my hands,
And all I could do was cry.

"It's ok Daddy."

Lily crawled out of her blankets,
And came towards me,
And embraced me in her tiny arms,
Holding onto me,
Still unsure why I'm like this,

And besides her small warmth,
I felt a shadow of shame hover above me.
Shame for not being strong,
And weak that my daughter had to comfort me,
When I should have been comforting her.

Time Flies

It's been a year since you last walked on earth,
Been 12 months since you ascended to the sky,
Been 365 days since I broke down into pieces,
Been 8760 hours since I flooded my house with tears,
Been 525,600 minutes since I was engulfed in
emptiness,
But still every second I am missing you,
And every minute I think of when I'll see you again.

Through The Rough

Around her are guns pointed at her,
Held by the hands of people who always tried to ruin
her,
Locking their deadly laser eyes upon her,
But she doesn't fidget.

She stands strong,
With cuts on her legs,
Bruises on her skin,
Blood on her lips,
Dirt on her face,

And a thundering heart that never frays.

"Aren't you cold?" "I like the rain."

The rain kisses my skin,
Devours me in love,
Cleanses my mind,
And rids all pain away,
For one sacred second.

Living Young

Hear the silence.
Feel the chaos.
Taste the lightning.
Breathe in the smoke
Of the flames of our youth.
Let it burn on your skin.
Every great memory,
Every sad tragedy,
Every moment of nothingness,
Let it ignite inside you.
Let the wildfire in you spread.
Let the fire run in your veins,
And let it nurture you into something better tomorrow.

I CAN HEAR YOU

You've been saying my name in vain,
Spreading lies while painting yourself as a fool,
And acting like I am nothing,
But compared to you I'm everything.

Remember

If my heart stops right now,
How would you remember me?

Would you remember me as a feeble person that never learned how to stand,
Or would you remember me as a courageous person that could stand against giants?

Would you remember me as a cruel person that brought turmoil wherever I went,
Or would you remember me as a sweet soul that can make people smile and laugh?

Would you remember me as a wilted flower buried in concrete,
Or would you remember me as a flourishing garden that colored the darkest days?

Would you remember me as a sick little bird that never flew,
Or would you remember me as a beautiful raven that soars the skies?

Would you only remember me as a walking creature with nothing special,

Or would you remember me as a person that has touched the stars?

Would you remember me as a ghost that only haunts empty places,
Or would you remember me as a soul who could light up the room?

Honestly I wouldn't know how I would remember
myself if I was someone else.
I wouldn't know if it would be good or bad to have me saved in your memory.

I do hope when I go you remember all the good days we shared,
But when you look at me like that I have no idea what you're thinking.

My Mine

Using an old shovel,
And a worn out pickaxe,
I've been digging through coal,
Hoping I could find more gold,
But it seems I can't find anything else,
And I got nothing more to feed the hungry wolves.

Thank you for reading.

Lightning Source UK Ltd.
Milton Keynes UK
UKHW020654040121
376386UK00014B/1452